SPECIAL FORCES/RANGER-UDT/SEAL
HAND-TO-HAND COMBAT/SPECIAL WEAPONS/
SPECIAL TACTICS SERIES

BASIC STICK FIGHTING
for COMBAT

SPECIAL FORCES/RANGER-UDT/SEAL HAND-TO-HAND COMBAT/ SPECIAL WEAPONS/ SPECIAL TACTICS SERIES

BASIC STICK FIGHTING
for COMBAT

by Michael D. Echanis

This book is dedicated to my Master Instructor, the Supreme Grand Master of Hwa Rang Do, Joo Bang Lee. Only through his great patience and vast knowledge has this been possible. I am forever dedicated to him and to Hwa Rang Do, for through his example and the teachings of his warrior's wisdom, one may discover the vast and infinite universe of knowledge within us all.

©1978 by Michael D. Echanis
All rights reserved
Printed in the United States of America
Library of Congress Catalog Card Number: 78-65738
Reproduction without permission is strictly prohibited

ISBN-10: 0-89750-059-8
ISBN-13: 978-0-89750-059-3

Twenty-seventh printing 2007

WARNING

BLACK BELT BOOKS
A Division of **OHARA** PUBLICATIONS, INC.
World Leader in Martial Arts Publications

ABOUT THE AUTHOR

MICHAEL D. ECHANIS was the developer and former Senior Instructor for the Special Forces/Ranger Hand-to-Hand Combat/Special Weapons School for instructors and the former Senior Instructor for the UDT-21, SEAL-2 Hand-to-Hand Combat/Special Weapons School for instructors. He presented seminars, demonstrations and advanced training to unconventional warfare experts from all over the world. His system of training has been termed by BLACK BELT magazine as "one of the most effective systems of hand-to-hand combat in the modern world." *Soldier of Fortune* magazine has termed him as "one of the leading experts in hand-to-hand combat in the world today."

Mr. Echanis was once a Special Forces Ranger and was privately tutored by Joo Bang Lee, the Supreme Grand Master of hwarang-do. He specialized in Un Shin Bup, the art of invisibility, the Korean counterpart to Japanese Ninjitsu and termed for modern military use as sentry stalking, silent killing. He was the first American Sul Sa in the history of Korean martial arts.

At the time of his death in Nicaragua in 1978, Mr. Echanis was studying the advanced mental aspects of hwarangdo that apply to ki, internal energy. He demonstrated his ability to utilize and control the five types of mental, physical power utilized in combat by hwarangdo warriors for over 2,000 years. Similar to the ancient testings of North American Indian warriors, hwarang warriors equally test themselves in breaking the barrier of changing from man to warrior.

Mr. Echanis demonstrated no pain or bleeding when the flesh of his neck and arms was pierced with needles suspending buckets of water. He had cars and military vehicles driven over his body while in a prone position. He demonstrated his ability to make his body immovable so that 100 soldiers could not lift or move him. He seemingly turned his body to steel as cement was crushed upon his chest while he lay on a bed of nails or while he received focused blows to vital portions of his body, as demonstrated by holding an ax blade to the throat and other portions of the body and receiving full-focused blows with a 2"-x-4" to the edge of the blade. The fifth, perhaps the most difficult to attain, is controlling this power directly with your mind and directing it to individual parts of the body and finally extending it outside the physical body through thought in conjunction with a special breathing technique. Mr. Echanis demonstrated this technique and utilized it in his study of Kookup Hwal Bub, the study of acupressure and acupuncture as utilized to revive an injured person during combat.

Mr. Echanis studied the advanced portions of Chuem Yan Sul, the ancient ability of Buddhist priests to focus the mind through concentration, sometimes termed hypnosis.

Mr. Echanis headed a Special Research Group of former Special Forces Rangers and UDT/SEAL Hand-to-Hand Combat experts who have developed a new system and approach to teaching, as directed by the guidelines of military instruction. Using the 2,000-year-old index of knowledge and battlefield experience utilized by hwarang warriors of Korea, this system of hand-to-hand combat/special weapons and special tactics has been tested and evaluated by unconventional warfare experts all over the world and the quality and professionalism of the program and its instruction is a reflection of the late Mr. Echanis himself.

Ohara Publications

HWARANGDO
ITS KOREAN HISTORY AND INTRODUCTION TO AMERICA

The present nation of Korea was once divided into three kingdoms. They were Koguryu, Paekche and Silla. Koguryu was the largest, at least in the beginning. It occupied the entire territory of present-day Manchuria as well as the northern part of the Korean peninsula.

In the fifth century, Koguryu made a bid to take over its two smaller neighbors. Paekche was almost overrun and forced to move its capital southward. Silla was constantly harassed. But here an unusual phenomenon was taking place that would one day make Silla the leading Korean kingdom.

Silla didn't break under the military pressure of Koguryu. Rather, the kingdom united and created new institutions to make it a formidable fighting machine. Foremost among the new institutions was the Hwarang. It included a core of young men of nobility who would produce the generals, statesmen and other leaders.

The great period of the united Silla was from 661—935 A.D. It was a time of immense development. Says martial arts historian Sang Kyu Shim, "The Hwarang entered a monumental period of peace, prosperity and development, inventing movable type 200 years before Gutenberg. It [Silla] also became a profoundly Buddhist country, printing lengthy Buddhist scriptures and constructing countless Buddhist temples and sculptures throughout the country."

Prior to 57 B.C., in the peninsula now known as Korea, a group called Won Hwa, a group of women, met for philosophical and intellectual discussions. This group was the ancient forerunner of hwarangdo.

At the time when Silla was being threatened by its larger and stronger neighbor, Koguryu, the people and government of Silla organized under the leadership of the Supreme Buddhist Monk Won Kwang Bopsa, a school of intellectual pursuits and martial arts thinking. This school came to be known as the Hwarang, or "Flower of Manhood." To this temple school, the king of Silla sent his sons and trusted soldiers to be trained in the philosophical codes and martial arts techniques developed by Won Kwang Bopsa.

Because of the martial arts training and particularly the philosophical and moral codes taught by the founders of the hwarangdo system, the tiny country of Silla eventually overcame the strength and size of its neighbors, Paekche and Koguryu, and ruled the peninsula known as Korea for many centuries.

Two of the Hwarang warriors, Kui San and Chu Hwang, were

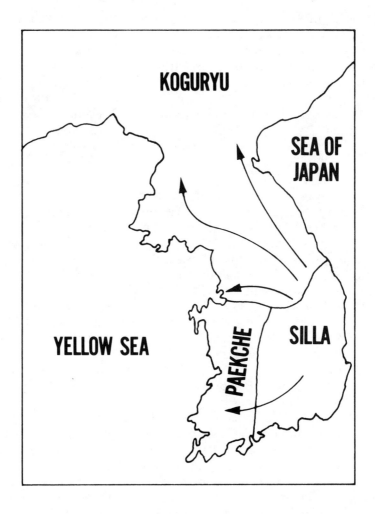

instrumental in obtaining from Won Kwang Bopsa a set of five rules by which they could govern their lives and purify their minds. Adding these rules to the virtues practiced by hwarangdo students already, the warriors had an all-encompassing set of guidelines by which they could conduct themselves properly as martial artists and as human beings. This set of guidelines is still remembered and practiced today by students of hwarangdo:

FIVE RULES:	NINE VIRTUES:
1. Loyalty to one's country.	1. Humanity
2. Loyalty to one's parents.	2. Honor
3. Trust and brotherhood among friends.	3. Courtesy
4. Courage never to retreat in the face of the enemy.	4. Knowledge
	5. Trust and Friendship
5. Justice never to take a life without cause.	6. Kindness
	7. Wisdom
	8. Loyalty
	9. Courage

From the earliest period in Korea, Won Kwang Bopsa's monastery was simultaneously a temple for the teaching of religious beliefs and a college for the instruction of higher learning as well as a gymnasium for the practice of the martial arts. It became a kind of spiritual/physical West Point for the intelligentsia of Silla. The Hwarang became the Korean version of the code of Bushido, popular in Japan.

Here, Won Kwang Bopsa and other priests trained many of the leading generals of the royal family. The establishment of the military/religious school led to the development of the Hwarang warriors who became legendary fighters. This ferocious fighting spirit led to the successful unification of Korea under Sill rule. Among the famous Hwarang warriors was General Yoo Sin Kim (595—673 A.D.).

During the Yi Dynasty (1392—1910 A.D.), the martial arts and the hwarangdo code fell into decline. The purely intellectual arts rose in stature and official recognition. With it came a dynastic policy of "favoring the arts and despising arms."

This led to the banishment of the warriors, with some taking refuge in Buddhist temples. There the art was preserved for centuries until the modern period. Much like the monks and monasteries were centers of learning during the so-called European Dark Ages, the Buddhist monks and temples in Korea preserved what they could of both the physical and religious aspects of hwarangdo.

Hwarangdo remained in Korean temples until the early 1950s. At that time, two Korean brothers, Joo Bang and Joo Sang Lee, began to study the art. They would soon bring it to the Korean population and later, America.

The Lee brothers were born in the 1930s. Their father was a martial artist, having black belts in judo and kendo, the only martial arts available under the Japanese Occupation. Father Lee began the boys' martial arts training early, training them at home as early as the age of two years old.

At the age of five, Joo Bang and Joo Sang were enrolled in the So Gwang Sa Buddhist Temple for religious and martial arts training, this temple being the current residence of the Grand Master of hwarangdo, a monk named Suahm Dosa.

In 1950, the Lee family moved to the southern tip of Korea, and the boys were enrolled in the Yang Mi Ahm temple on O Dae Mountain, where Suahm Dosa had also relocated. The Lee brothers' training continued here, and in 1960, they received permission from their master to open a hwarangdo school in public, the first one in modern times, in Seoul, Korea. Subsequent to the opening of the first school in Seoul, the Korea Hwarang-Do Federation was granted a government permit to function as a martial arts association in Korea.

In 1968, Joo Bang Lee was presented with the Lion's Award as the Martial Artist of the Year. 1968 was also the year hwarangdo first came to the Western world. In that year, Master Joo Sang Lee came to the United States and opened a hwarangdo school in Huntington Park, California.

In 1969, Master Suahm Dosa died and the position of Grand Master was passed to Joo Bang Lee. This position made Joo Bang Lee the Grand Master of hwarangdo in an unbroken line of succession lasting over 1,800 years, directly descending from the two warriors and hwarangdo masters of Won Kwang Bopsa's time, Kui San and Chu Hwang. In 1972, Joo Bang Lee came to the United States to spread the art of hwarangdo. Today, there are approximately 56 hwarangdo schools in Korea and another 38 in the United States and Europe. Joo Bang Lee is the Grand Master of hwarangdo and President of the International Hwarang-Do Federation, and his brother Joo Sang Lee is the Head Master and Chairman of the International Hwarang-Do Federation.

HWA RANG DO

THE GRAND MASTER OF HWARANGDO
JOO BANG LEE

道主 李柱邦

Mr. Echanis is privately tutored by the Grand Master of Hwarang-do, Joo Bang Lee, in the secret portions of the inner arts.

SPECIAL OPERATIONS,
RESEARCH AND DEVELOPMENT GROUP
SENIOR ADVISORS AND HEAD INSTRUCTORS
OFFICE FOR THE STUDY OF CONFLICT AND TACTICS

SENIOR ADVISOR NAVY/SPECIAL WARFARE STUDIES

> MASTER CHIEF PETTY OFFICER NISSLEY/
> U.S. NAVAL ADVISOR USAJFKCENMA
> UNITED STATES NAVY

SENIOR ADVISOR ARMY SPECIAL WARFARE STUDIES

> MASTER SERGEANT
> JAKOVENKO/5TH SPECIAL FORCES GROUP
> UNITED STATES ARMY

SENIOR ADVISOR PSYCHO-PHYSICAL STUDIES

> MASTER SERGEANT
> JACKSON/HEAD INSTRUCTOR
> SPECIAL FORCES MEDICAL SCHOOL
> FORMER VIETNAM P.O.W.

HEAD INSTRUCTOR

> SPECIAL FORCES/HAND-TO-HAND COMBAT
> SPECIAL WEAPONS INSTRUCTORS' TEAM
> SERGEANT SANDERS/5TH SPECIAL FORCES GROUP
> UNITED STATES ARMY

HEAD INSTRUCTOR

> 82ND AIRBORNE RAIDER RECONDO/HAND-TO-HAND COMBAT
> SPECIAL WEAPONS INSTRUCTORS' TEAM
> STAFF SERGEANT O'NEAL, RANGER INSTRUCTOR
> UNITED STATES ARMY

HEAD INSTRUCTOR

> UDT-SEAL/HAND-TO-HAND COMBAT
> SPECIAL WEAPONS INSTRUCTORS' TEAM
> 1ST CLASS PETTY OFFICER PAAINA
> SEAL TEAM II
> UNITED STATES NAVY

HEAD INSTRUCTOR

> FORCE RECON/HAND-TO-HAND COMBAT
> SPECIAL WEAPONS INSTRUCTORS' TEAM
> STAFF SERGEANT O'GRADY
> 2 FORCE RECON UNITED STATES MARINE CORPS

HWARANGDO
AND ITS RELATIONSHIP TO HAND-TO-HAND COMBAT

Hand-to-hand combat is as old as the human race. Fighting techniques developed as warfare became more organized, and the different fighting styles which evolved were modified and influenced by the different cultures and traditions of the period. But only in Asia did different styles of empty-handed combat become an art regarded as secrets of the State or harbored within the walls of the religious monasteries. The Asian fighting arts were frequently connected with religious movements of Buddhism. Within the Buddhist religion there were both a fighting and a pacifist sect.

Hwarangdo differs from many other of the more familiar martial arts in that it is designed purely as a way of deadly fighting. It is not intended to be an educational system, a competitive sport, a form of self-improvement, although it can be all these things. Consistent with its origins as a fighting system for feudal warriors, hwarangdo includes all forms of personal combat, as well as training in the use of hand weapons and instruction in revival techniques. Its advanced stages encompass the occult mental disciplines of the inner arts.

Hwarangdo does not fall either into the hard, linear category of martial art, or into the soft, circular category. Rather, it includes both hard and soft, both straight-line and circular. Hwarangdo is considered a dialectical form of combat, inasmuch as it contains opposite or contradictory elements within its single unity, and derives its strength from the dynamic interbalance between the two. This dialectical conception flows from Asian cosmology, symbolized by the swirling circle in the South Korean flag, which holds that all opposing forces of the universe, uhm and yang in Korean (yin and yang in Chinese), are indivisible.

Hard and Soft Styles

Uhm symbolizes softness and darkness, and is represented in the martial arts in the soft fighting styles. Its power is that of gently flowing water that changes the shape of stone. Its typical motion is circular, with the force of a whip, or a rock whirled on a string, and its tendency is to unite and combine to close in.

Yang symbolizes hardness and brightness, and is represented in the arts in the hard, linear forms of fighting. Its strength is that of steel or rock, and its typical motion is straight lines and angles, with force derived from leverage. Its tendency is to maintain distance between opponents.

Hwarangdo incorporates the elements of uhm along with the elements of yang. Its karate-like techniques involve straight punches and kicks of the familiar type, but they also include spectacular circular spin-kicks, some traveling as much as 540 degrees before impact, a build-up of tremendous centrifugal force. These kicks can be aimed at the body or at the head, or they can whip in at mat level to cut an opponent's feet out from under him.

A punch or a kick from an opponent, or a blow from a weapon, may be met in kind, or it can be answered with a breaking of joints, a throw, or an attack against the opponent's nerves or acupuncture points. It can be met with a hard block and finished with a punch or a kick, or it can be met with a loose-wristed deflection similar to the Hawaiian lima-lama techniques, trapped by the flexible hand, and finished with a throw or a joint-dislocation.

Hwarangdo includes a complete discipline of throwing techniques, some similar to the body throws of judo, others similar to the pain throws of aikido. But hwarangdo throws are always executed in their combat, or disabling form, never in their sport form.

Hwarangdo training also includes counter-throws, finger-pressure techniques (more than 300) applied against nerve or acupuncture points, 30 different choking techniques and a system of ground fighting or matwork based to some extent on ancient Mongolian grappling.

Weapons training includes kumdo (Korean kendo), both with the bamboo sword and with the live blade, stick-fighting with all lengths of sticks, short-sword and spear techniques, knife throwing and the throwing of dirks, pointed stars, stones, etcetera.

At advanced black belt levels, students begin to learn the healing arts of acupuncture and finger-pressure revival.

When hwarangdo students reach fourth-degree black belt, they may qualify for training in a martial art completely different from the techniques they have learned before, consisting of 36 categories of killing techniques.

HWARANGDO'S DYNAMIC TECHNIQUES

Hwarangdo techniques are founded on three basic divisions of power—inner, exterior and mental. Aspects of each are taught as the student progresses in his training. Hwarangdo includes all forms of personal combat. It is a true yin/yang martial art. Both hard/soft and straight-line/circular forms and techniques are found in hwarangdo.

In advanced studies, hwarangdo deals with mental disciplines and becomes an "inner art." The techniques and principles are effective for such diverse needs as personal self-defense, mob control and mental discipline.

On the purely physical and technical level, the knowledgeable practitioner will spot forms similar to a broad range of martial arts. Below is a breakdown of the techniques in which hwarangdo students are instructed:

A. INNER POWER TECHNIQUES (NEGONG):

These are developed by controlled breathing and concentrating or focusing the ki at a single point. It is said to be the essence of power behind kicking and punching. The techniques are broken down in 21 subdivisions:

1. Joint techniques. These are self-defense techniques directed at the opponent's joints.

2. Throwing techniques.

3. Breathing exercises. These are learned in order to develop power by breath control.

4. Head techniques. These encompass techniques for using the head as a weapon.

5. Hand-breaking techniques. These include self-defense movements *against* hand grabs.

6. Kicking techniques. These are based on three basic kicking types: snapping, thrust and circular.

7. Finger-pressure techniques.

8. Choking techniques.

9. Rolling techniques.

10. Self-defense techniques from a seated position.

11. Self-defense techniques from a prone position.

12. Punching and striking techniques.

13. Forms. There are 30 forms or *hyung*, patterns or series of movements used as training forms so that the student can learn techniques.

14. Breaking boards or stones. These techniques stem from the combination of physical and mental power or outer and inner strength concentrated at a single point.

15. Tearing of flesh with bare hands.

16. Unarmed self-defense against knife attack.

17. Counter-defense against throwing techniques.

18. Counter-defense against kicking attacks.

19. Counter-defense against punching attacks.

20. Come-along or hand control techniques.

21. Defense against more than two opponents.

B. EXTERIOR POWER TECHNIQUES (WAY-GONG):

This section of instruction deals with what is commonly known in kung fu or karate as weapons training. Hwarangdo students learn the use of the sword, stick, spear, short sword, knife and other exotic weapons, such as throwing dirks, pointed stars and stones.

C. MENTAL POWER TECHNIQUES (SHIN-GONG):

These techniques directly affect the "life energy force" of the human body. They are divided into six areas:

1. **KIAPSUL.** Here a combination of physical, mental and breathing power plus concentration

is learned in order to break solid objects more efficiently.

2. **KYUK PA SUL.** Extracting mind power. Refers to the capacity of the mind to extract latent power inherent in every human. The mind may possess a 100-percent potential, but the normal condition is a person who uses only a small portion of this power. It is possible with the proper training, according to the Lee brothers, to develop the full potential.

3. **CHUEM YAN SUL.** Technique of putting a person to sleep.

4. **KOOKUP HWAL BUB.** Use of acupuncture to revive an injured person.

5. **CHIMGOO SUL PUP.** Acupuncture as a medicinal science.

6. **GUN SHIN PUP.** The art of concealing oneself in front of others. It employs a combination of distraction, suggestion, stealth and camouflage used by spies and assassins, such as the celebrated Japanese Ninja.

THE THEORY OF KI POWER IN HWARANGDO

Grand Master Joo Bang Lee explains the theory surrounding ki power in this way. The *danjun* area, or seat of this power in the human body is located one to three inches below the navel. It is comprised of three points: *ki hae*, located one inch below the navel; *kwan won*, two inches below, and *suk mon*, three inches below the navel.

This danjun is the center from which all life energy, or power, emanates. Lee says that a human being cannot even move one finger without the power from danjun. Although all people have this power, not everyone has the same level of control over it. But with the proper training in special techniques devised and developed by hwarangdo masters over the last 2,000 years, it is possible to increase the level of ki power over which a person has control.

This ki power in hwarangdo functions in five different ways. One way is to make the body heavy. Another is to make the body light. The third is to make the body feel like steel. The fourth is to make the body numb, so that no pain is felt. The fifth, and perhaps the most difficult to attain, is to control this power directly with your mind in individual parts of the body and even outside the physical body. An example of this last form of ki power would be to use the power to make your arm or leg move faster than is possible by purely physical means, as in the execution of a punch or kick.

In American schools, students are taught to develop ki power through the following two basic methods:

1. Danjun ki (air ki): The scientific application of controlled breathing techniques to build up ki power.

2. Shin ki (mental ki): The use of mental techniques taught through meditation to gain mastery over unlimited amounts of ki power purely through the medium of mind control. Examples of this method occurring spontaneously without prior training are the many documented cases of persons who, under extreme fear or stress circumstances, lift or move an object which would normally require the strength of ten people, such as a mother lifting a car under which her child is trapped.

Hwarangdo ki theory also delves into the study of what is said to be the movement in and out of the body of the "spirit" or "life force," particularly that movement which occurs near or at the time of death. In the region of the eighth to tenth vertebrae (from the top of the spine), hwarangdo masters explain, is a "door," or exit point, where the spirit leaves the body at the time of death. This door is called *myung mon sa hwa hyel.*

The importance of ki theory is relevant to a basic tenet of hwarangdo training—the belief that the martial artist must be able to heal injuries and illness because he has the power to cause them. Therefore, students undergo medical training (acupuncture, herbal medicine, bone setting, etcetera), prior to learning the more dangerous and deadly black belt techniques.

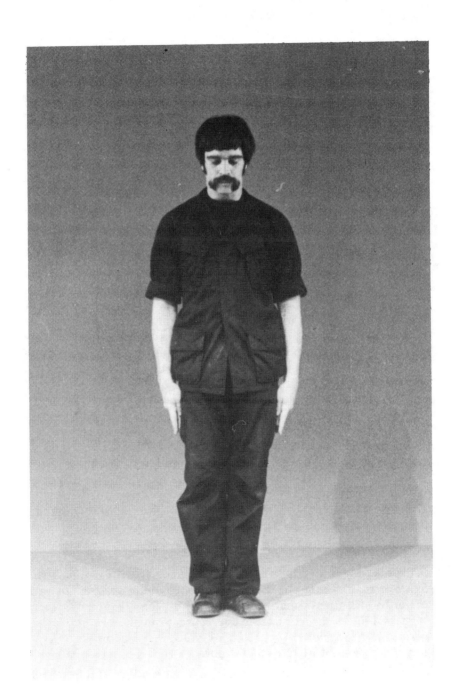

INTRODUCTION

The stick is probably the most available "field expedient," weapon to which a soldier has access, and as a combat weapon, it becomes usable for everything from riot control, prisoner control, to an extremely lethal close-quarter combat weapon. The stick can at one moment be a cane, and the next moment be breaking a man's wrist, arm or neck. In this context we will primarily deal with the stick and its use in combat as a weapon and for survival. Various sizes and different techniques will give you the basis for evaluation and re-adjustment, so that each technique will conform to you and your mental/physical abilities. One important factor in your evaluation of the stick as a weapon, in contrast and comparison to the knife, is the stick's focus of attack upon the bony protrusions and nerve centers of the human anatomy, while the knife attacks cutting and slashing veins, arteries, muscles and tendons of the body. In the study of close-quarter combat and its scientific application of technique during actual attack, the focus of mental/physical contact must be directed to vital portions of the human anatomy, and by the simple and correct application of technique and mental focus of power, the smallest man can become a lethal weapon to the largest of assailants. A weapon in the hand of a trained individual is the integral difference between a lethal and a nonlethal, close-quarter combat technique.

An example of applying common sense to this type of situation is the use of an ashtray at close quarters a lethal combat weapon. The edge of the glass curvature, the outer portion of the weapon, becomes the focus point of attack, when directed to bony protrusions of the enemy's anatomy such as finger joints, knuckles, bony portions of the upper hand, wrist, elbow, collarbone, jawbone, bridge of the nose or temple. A well-focused strike with this *simple, commonly-found weapon*, will deliver a disabling or extremely lethal blow in a crucial self-defense situation.

The writing pen or a hardwood pencil is another example of a *simple, commonly-found weapon*, which can be a lifesaving factor in certain life-or-death situations, or in the face of physical violence or rape. There are many methods to injure an assailant with merely a "Bic pen," hardwood pencil, a set of keys or a comb, such as a direct thrust into the eyes, throat, jugular vein or clavicle region of the enemy. These harsh methods of reaction are necessary in life-and-death, hand-to-hand combat encounters, and only those who are willing to remain calm and act decisively, will survive these types of violent encounters.

Common sense, and the awareness of readily available, natural and man-made weapons in your immediate surroundings and their application of attack to vital areas of the human anatomy are the keys to mastering survival in close-quarter combat. It can be as simple as throwing hot coffee in the eyes of the enemy to gain that needed split second for reaction.

The stick is invaluable in the sense of "common sense," and its application of attack to the anatomy of the enemy. Study the *"vital striking chart"* on page 27, and memorize these critical points of the human anatomy.

The following chapters will include sections on the use of the baton, double short stick, (a small oak stick, 10 inches in length and one inch in diameter, termed the "Bone Breaker,") and a special chapter on cane techniques demonstrated by my master, the supreme grandmaster of hwa rang do, Joo Bang Lee.

STICK TRAINING

In weapons training, the most important factor in your proficiency and use of any weapon is your ability to form the weapon into an extension of your body and mind.

Second, techniques of attack and counterattack must become conditioned reflexes and second nature to the stick trainee.

Third, vital portions of the anatomy must be focused upon during attack, and each vital point must be memorized and studied, so as to imbed the imprint of these points and their positions within the human anatomy, upon the subconscious mind. This will cause you to react physically with trained techniques in a natural order, flow of movement and power, to the critical point of the enemy's anatomy.

When these three basic principles have been unified into one precision movement of mind and body, all weapons will seem as *one*, and all natural and man-made objects within your surroundings will become available tools of survival.

GRIP OF THE WEAPON

The stick must *never* be constricted with an iron grip, but must become an extension of the force of the body and mind, with a firm but relaxed hand and wrist, guiding the flow with your index finger, much as a stream of light would seem from a flashlight or laser beam.

The stick may be grasped with one or two hands, depending upon the situation and the technique being used. The majority of the strength for gripping is focused in your last three fingers. The striking-hand-grip allows you to snap a shocking, sharp blow to a vital point of the bony regions of the enemy's anatomy. This method of striking is best demonstrated in the "Bone Breaker," chapter .

Normally the stick is grasped approximately one-third of the distance, as measured from the *butt* to the *point*; much like choking up on a baseball bat, and adjusted to your ability to *feel* comfortable with the stick, allowing it to become an extension of your *force*. You must *feel* relaxed with the weapon, as it is merely an extension of yourself.

The stick or baton should never exceed the length of your forearm or tip of your elbow at a 90-degree flexion.

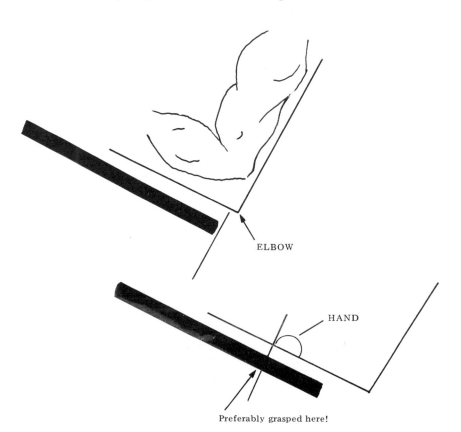

ELBOW

HAND

Preferably grasped here!

Measure your grip from the butt of the baton and tip of your elbow to a point between your forearm and wrist that allows you maximum range of motion and full ability to focus your power, yet remain relaxed.

STRIKING

There are three basic methods of striking:
1. Thrusting
2. Snapping/Shocking
3. Whipping

Strikes and contact are made with the tip of the baton, the butt of the weapon or the edge of the curvature. In training for stick fighting, remain simple, and focus your power and techniques to vital points of the enemy's anatomy.

Stand relaxed, feet approximately shoulder width apart, step forward as if performing a karate punch, bringing the stick forward as an extension of your body, arm, wrist or hand and then *punch*. Perform this simple exercise to familiarize yourself with the *feel* of the weapon.

As you practice this method of familiarization, imagine and visualize upon your mental screen a target identical in height and weight. Practice striking at vital points such as the eyes, throat, sternum, nipples, solar plexus or floating ribs, hips, pelvic bone, groin and thigh.

Short, shocking blows are performed in a six-inch to 12-inch snapping/shocking motion, snapping the stick at the point of contact, retracting the stick quickly so that the enemy cannot grasp the weapon, and so that you will be prepared for your next strike. Follow through the point of contact three inches to six inches. As you retract, inhale quickly and deeply, gaining power for your next strike.

Whipping actions should be performed in figure "eights" and circles and are normally directed to the exterior regions of the anatomy, striking with the curvature of the stick. Targets are the head, neck, wrist and arms, body, knees and the leg below the knee. Force and power are generated by centrifugal energy, directed and extended with tremendous follow-through as the circle is completed, and the weapon follows through the point of contact.

STICK FIGHTING FOR COMBAT

Efficient use of the stick as a weapon in combat depends upon one important factor, *interval*. Interval is the distance between two combatants in relationship to the length of the stick or baton, for once body-to-body interval and contact are made, the use of the baton is decreased tremendously, and can actually hinder your performance. The use of the baton at close quarters in a tight-crowd situation, where your interval is six inches to 18 inches from the assailant, can become extremely hazardous.

Here, in this tight interval, the short stick, "bone breaker," supercedes the use of the baton, and is a much more suitable weapon. Short, fast and maneuverable, the 10-inch short stick with its wrap-around cord, proves a formidable weapon and is very difficult to grasp. Equally, if you do not strike the enemy while at stick-length interval, then he may engage you in close-quarter striking and throwing techniques, striking or throwing you to the ground, rendering the stick useless, again, because the interval gap was not controlled.

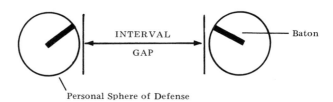

Personal Sphere of Defense

The combat soldier must envision upon his mental screen, a 360-degree sphere of defense surrounding him and the ground which he holds. The first portion of the enemy's anatomy to enter this 360-degree sphere of defense, such as a wrist in a striking technique, or a lower leg during a kick, must be struck with a snapping, shocking, thrusting motion, focusing through the point of contact mentally, and following through with a tremendous *shock* of physical power. Remain relaxed until contact, exhale forcefully, simultaneously tensing your lower abdomen and entire muscle structure, grasping firmly at the moment of contact with the final three fingers of your striking hand or hands.

VISUALIZATION AND BREATH CONTROL

VISUALIZATION

Mental visualization is extremely important, for the mind directs all force and power in the body.

Psychologists say that different colors have different, or create different emotional reactions in the human mind and body.

Focus your eyes upon a red piece of cloth. Now close your eyes and visualize the mental screen as completely red. Next, visualize yourself performing one of the techniques on your mental screen, and surround yourself and your image in the color *red*. Actually *see* mentally your physical actions and follow through. *One hundred percent emotional content* is essential for unification of the mind and body as one extended force of the universe, and our resource of energy, man's mind.

These are the principles of martial arts that exemplify life and death, the infinite universe and the link to the infinite, inner, universal power of man.

Many great warriors of Asian history were enlightened during their training or battles with their swords. The great swordmaster of Japan, Musashi, killed the majority of his opponents with a wooden training sword. Musashi said he was led to this inner-self and understanding, through the use of his sword or wooden stick. At the age of *62, never defeated in countless close-quarter combats with the sword* he returned to a cave in the mountain, where he trained relentlessly, writing his now-famous guide to strategy, *A Book of Five Rings*. This book can be applied directly to any type of weapons training and fighting, and is recommended for your study and the analyzation of any mental strategy.

BREATH CONTROL

Before striking, inhale deeply, forcing the air deep into the lower abdomen. Mentally you must simultaneously visualize the flow of air as a force and power, building up energy and air in the lower abdomen, physically and mentally. The extension of this force and inner power, is directed as you exhale, and follow through the point of contact. Mentally visualize the transference of power as a *light field*, extended from the ground, through the body and into the weapon itself. Extending through the weapon and point of contact, this force is directed by your physical movements, your breath control and mental visualization.

FOCUS OF ATTACK

The stick focuses its attack at one of five targets:
1. The top of the head
2. The side of the neck
3. The wrist
4. The body
5. The leg below the knee, including the knee itself.

Each target has a multiple variation of strikes, which are applied from eight different angles of attack.

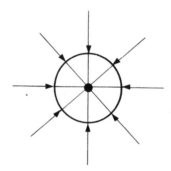

The mental/physical focus of movement is based upon the initial situation encountered. Targets of opportunity are based upon the defensive position of the enemy and the openings in his perimeter of defense. A straight-line thrust to the eyes, throat, sternum, solar plexus, pelvic bone or groin can be simple, initial strikes if you are first to attack.

In counterattack situations, strikes into the enemy's wrist, elbow, ankle, shin, knee, body or top of the head are appropriate.

If a man attacks you with a hand-held weapon, then the initial strike is to break the wrist of the attacking hand, disarming the weapon, disabling the enemy and denying him use of his hand and tool of attack. A groin kick can be simply sidestepped, and using a downward swing, similar to swinging a baseball bat, the stick strikes the kneecap, shinbone, ankle or instep of the enemy's attacking leg.

The enemy's own force and motion, acting as added velocity, increasing the shock at contact, will obviously be utilized against him.

Sharp blows to the nerve centers of the muscular anatomy, and hand thrusts with the point or butt of the stick serve to deliver the focus of the weapons attack to vital points of the enemy's anatomy. Some are used for momentary neutralization and control, while other points are considered killing zones. This type of technique is exemplified in the use of the 10-inch short, oak stick, and this type of attack is extremely lethal.

The use of the stick in combat is limited only by your imagination, and its availability as a field expedient weapon. To encompass stick fighting and this type of training is to enhance our chances of survival in close-quarter combat. The guerrilla-warfare expert is the soldier of ingenuity. Left many times with nothing but his environment to assist in his survival, he constantly must search his surroundings for those things which will assist in his survival. The jungle is like the sea, one moment in front of you, and the next engulfing you in its vastness.

Remain calm, don't panic, act decisively with the total focus of body and mind. This will be your best advantage in that moment when you are called upon to defend your life in a crucial life-and-death situation. *Win or Die*, are the terms of hand-to-hand combat.

VITAL STRIKING CHART

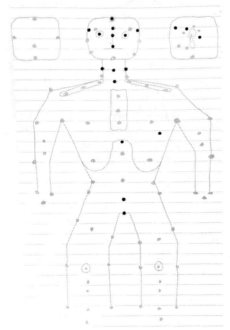

•critical points of the
human anatomy

CHAPTER ONE

THE BATON

The *BATON* is one of the most readily available weapons to which a soldier has access in the field. The *middle stick, baton, night stick, riot stick,* or *billy club* is a multifaceted weapon, and its average size of between 18 inches and 36 inches, creates this field-expedient readily-available tool of self-defense into one of those *common sense* vehicles of protection. It is easy to pick up a good stick, or when needed, a "BIG" stick.

When used properly, the baton is one of the most effective tools of control available in man's arsenal of hand-held weapons. Man has been using the stick since he began throwing rocks, as his first means of protection, and as a weapon to hunt game in his struggle ,for survival. In the days of hand-held laser guns, tranquilizer dart pistols, electrical laser shock weapons and sophisticated handguns, the baton or stick, is still one of the most effective weapons of control available. Inducing a minimum of physical injury, but the necessary force to restrain and control an assailant, the baton is excellent for prisoner control, or subduing a criminal, and as an alternate course to the handgun. The baton must be considered as a primary weapon for all policemen and security personnel, who may be faced with the situation of control during civil disturbances, riots or personal encounters, where sufficient restraint of force and injury are called upon to insure the safety of the civilian.

In the following chapter, I will focus upon several basic aspects in the use of the baton:
1. Basic free-form with the baton
2. Basic blocks
3. Basic strikes
4. Clearing the baton
5. Basic striking combinations
6. Disarming the baton once it has been grasped by the assailant

7. Striking, joint-locking, takedowns and controls with the baton

8. Choking with the baton.

These *BASIC* techniques will guide you into the basic knowledge so that you may search further and discover which will work best for you. Always perfect and refine the basics, the rest will come naturally and in time.

The baton is an excellent weapon for control, but the *baton* is a *weapon*, and is an extremely lethal tool of self-defense. In combat it can be used to kill, and when in the hands of a trained policeman, is a method of self-protection and control. The degree of force used, and the techniques applied will depend upon the situation and the ability of the soldier or policeman to remain calm, and react accordingly. This book was written for the special warfare soldier, the guerrilla fighter, but it has meaning for the person concerned with common-sense self-defense. Many techniques in the following chapters are considered lethal, and when applied correctly with the right amount of force, can kill the assailant or permanently injure him.

GREAT CAUTION must be taken when practicing with any *STICK*, and here, you must study for the purpose of restraint and control, but in combat, it will be your choice for survival. Hopefully, some of these techniques will provide some basis for this knowledge and your struggle to perfect your abilities to defend and survive.

The most important aspect of fighting with the baton, is *interval*. The enemy should be kept within striking distance, for once body-to-body contact is made, the baton becomes cumbersome and clumsy. Maintain control of the distance and movement of the enemy. Strike critical, hard points in the bony anatomy of the assailant or nerve centers for a paralyzing effect upon the attacker. Thrusts to the eyes, throat, solar plexus and groin, are extemely lethal, and must be considered primary targets during combat, and the last resort during methods of control. Strikes to the wrist, hands, knees, shins and ankles, are excellent methods of blocking, and should be executed once the enemy has penetrated your sphere of defense. Remember, the *baton* is a *weapon*, and due respect must be taken for its lethality and ability to induce injury. It will always remain extremely hazardous for your training partner, if great caution is not taken during training.

FREE FORM/FIGURE 8

**FREE FORM
DOUBLE ARM STRIKES**

CLEARING THE BATON FROM THE READY RELAXED POSITION

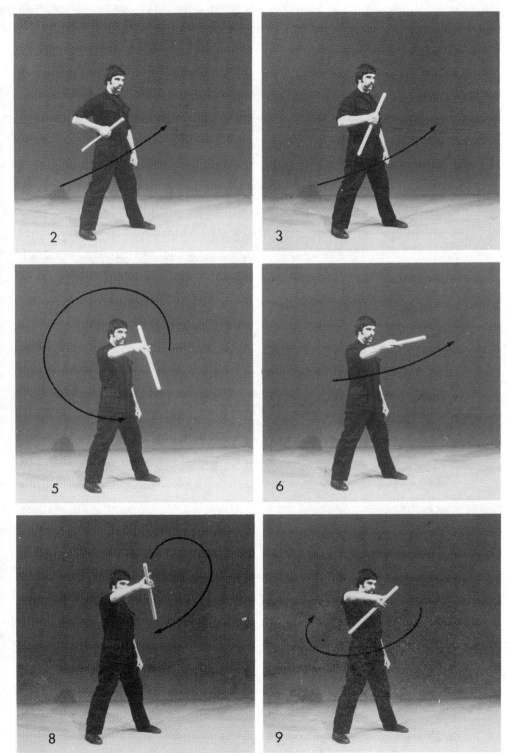

CONTINUED

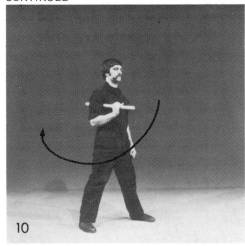

10

13

16

17

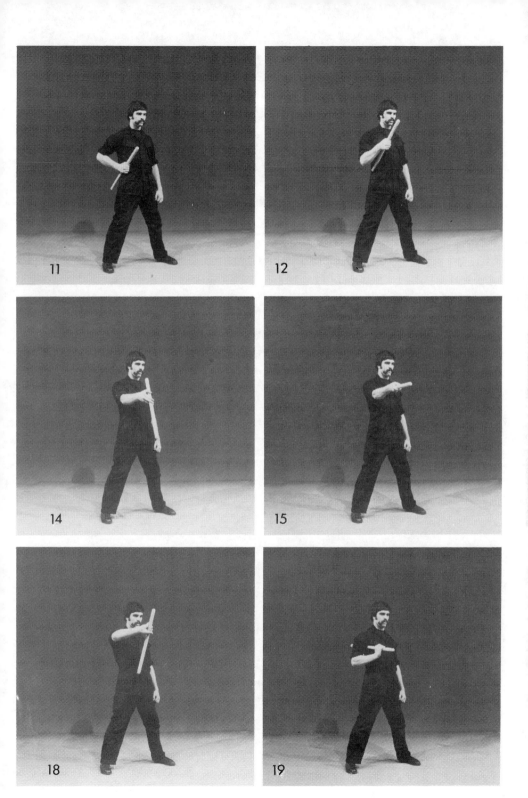

TWO-HANDED FREE FORM DRILL

2

3

5

6

8

9

CONTINUED

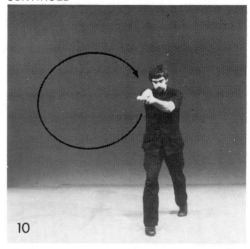

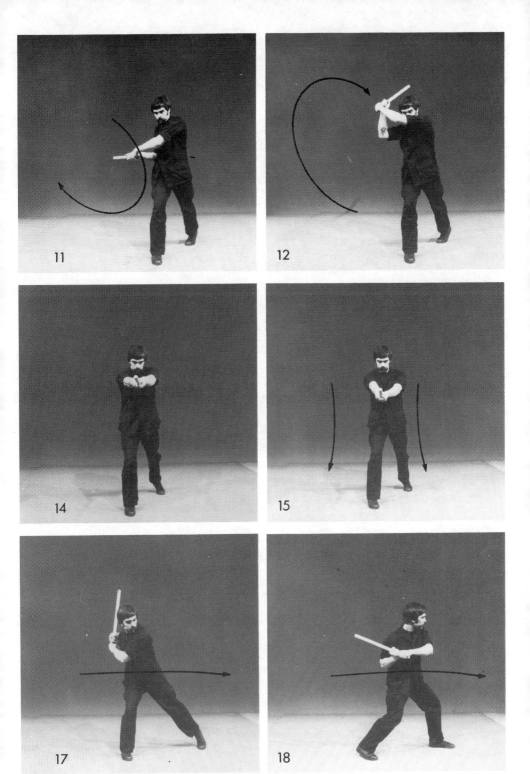

11

12

14

15

17

18

CONTINUED

19

21

24

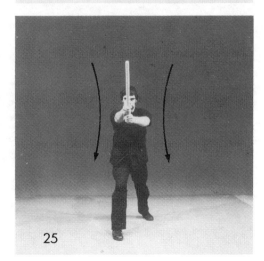

**FOUR
ONE-HANDED BLOCKS**

DOUBLE DOWNWARD
45-DEGREE ANGLE
BLOCKS

46

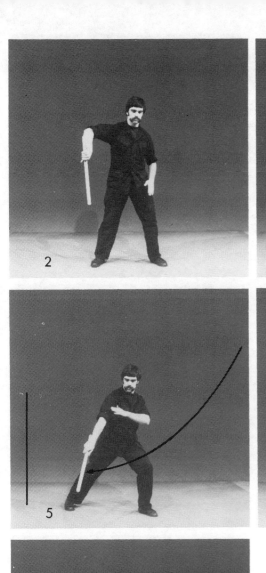

**FOUR
TWO-HANDED BLOCKS**

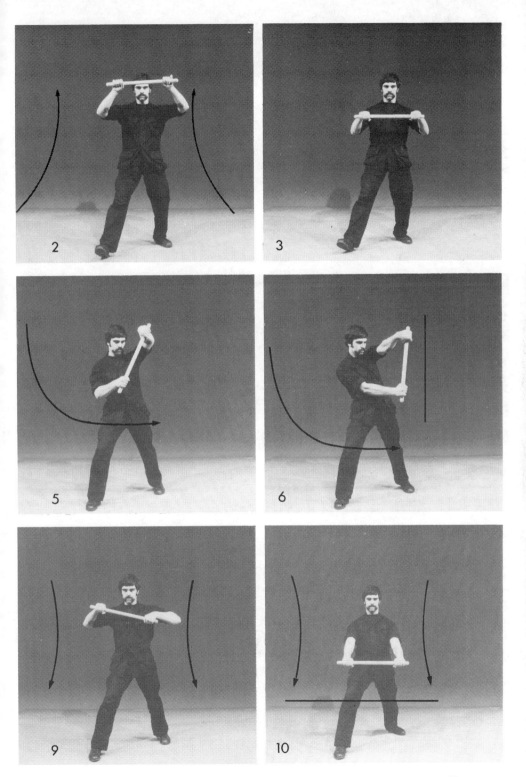

1

2

**TWO-HANDED
THRUST TO THE
SOLAR PLEXUS**

3

**TWO-HANDED
THRUST TO
THE THROAT**

TWO-HANDED
CROSS STRIKE
TO THE THROAT

BATON THRUST TO THE SOLAR PLEXUS FROM THE BELT POSITION

1

**BATON THRUST
TO THE THROAT
FROM THE
BELT POSITION**

2

3

4

WRIST STRIKE, HEAD STRIKE FROM THE READY RELAXED POSITION

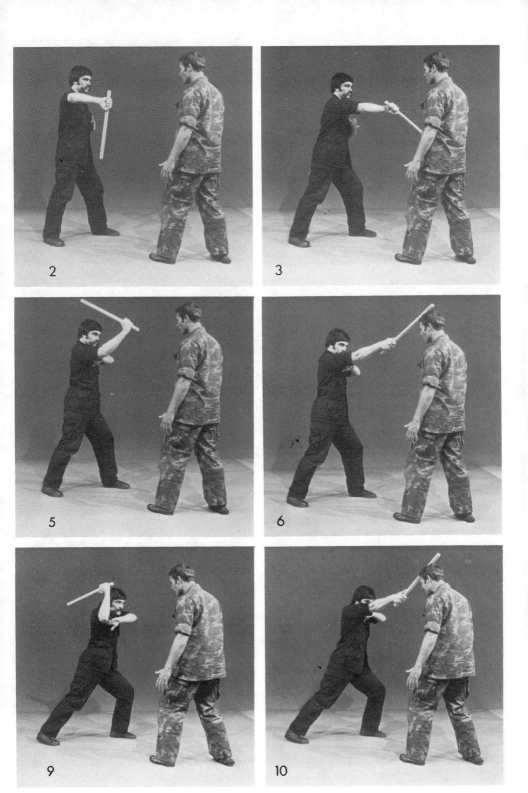

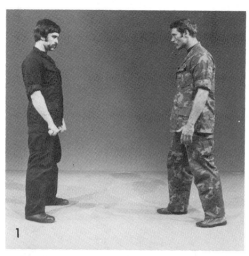

**TWO-HANDED THRUST
TO THE SOLAR PLEXUS
AND A DOUBLE
COLLARBONE STRIKE
FROM THE
READY COMBAT POSITION**

TWO-HANDED HIGH BLOCK WITH A STOMACH AND KIDNEY STRIKE FROM THE READY COMBAT POSITION

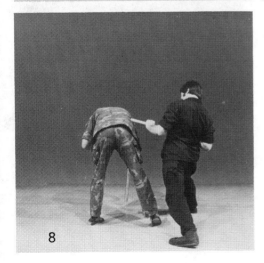

TWO-HANDED STRIKING BLOCK AGAINST AN ARMED ATTACK WITH A HEAD STRIKE AND LOWER LEG STRIKE

DOUBLE CIRCULAR
DISARMING TECHNIQUE
UTILIZED AGAINST AN
OPPONENT WHO GRASPS
THE BATON DURING
A DOWN STRIKE

SINGLE CIRCULAR
DISARMING TECHNIQUE
UTILIZED AGAINST A
TWO-HANDED GRASP AND
DEFENSE AGAINST A
DOWN STRIKE OF
THE BATON

A CHANGING HAND GRASP
WITH A SHOULDER THROW
AS THE OPPONENT
GRASPS THE WEAPON
ON A DOWN STRIKE

**A SLIDING GROIN KICK
WITH A STOMACH THROW**

1

4

7

8

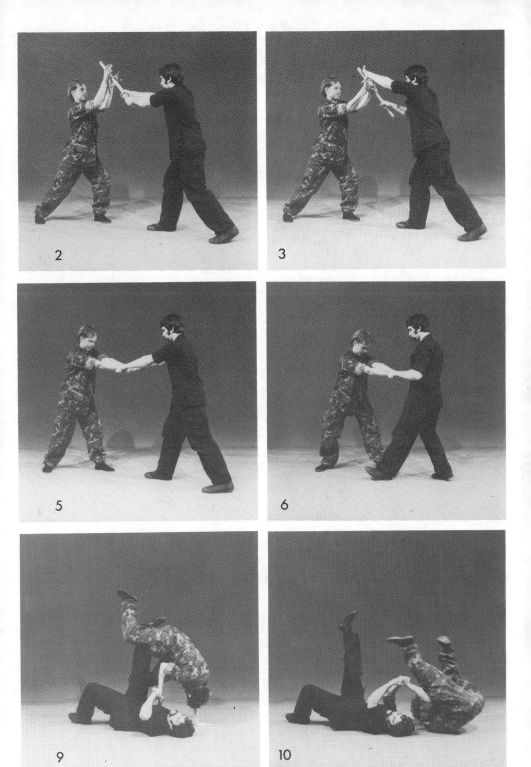

AN OUTSIDE CIRCULAR WRIST-BREAKING THROW

1

4

5

8

9

**A NECK STRIKE WITH AN
OUTSIDE CIRCULAR
ARM BAR, TAKEDOWN
AND CONTROL**

**NECK STRIKE,
ELBOW STRIKE,
OVER-THE-SHOULDER
ARM BAR**

STOMACH THRUST WITH AN
INSIDE HALF-NELSON
APPLIED WITH THE BATON,
TAKEDOWN AND CONTROL

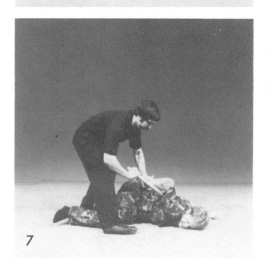

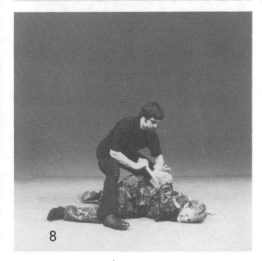

STOMACH THRUST, INSIDE
ARM BAR WITH A SLIDING
HIP THROW IN CONJUNCTION
WITH A BATON ARM BAR
APPLIED TO THE ELBOW
AFTER THE TAKEDOWN
FOR CONTROL

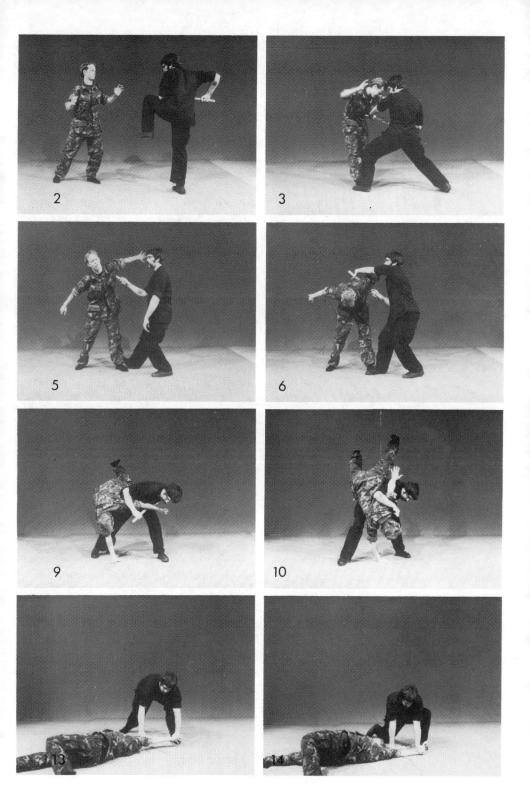

A STRIKING WRIST BLOCK,
NECK STRIKE, OUTSIDE
CIRCULAR LOWER LEG STRIKE,
LEG STRIKE TWO WITH A
SPINNING DOWN STRIKE
TO THE BACK OF THE HEAD

CONTINUED

10

13

16

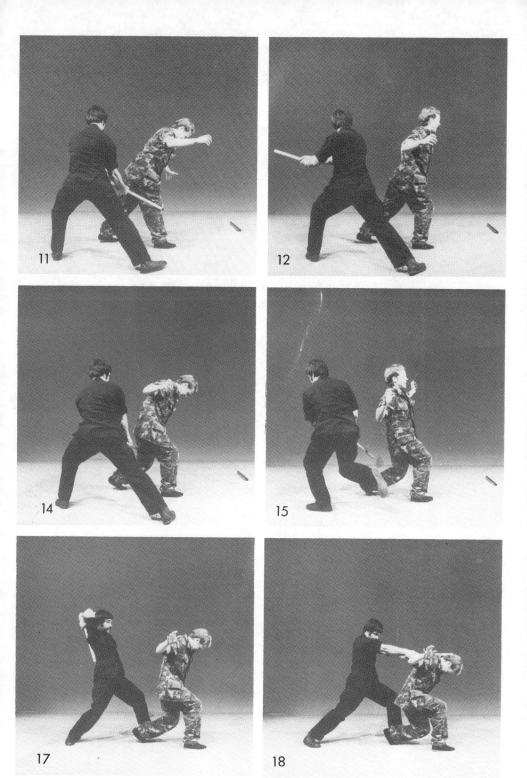

**NECK STRIKE WITH AN
OUTSIDE CIRCULAR SLEEPER
CHOKE, APPLIED WITH
THE BATON**

2

3

5

6

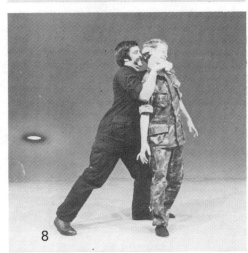

8

9

89

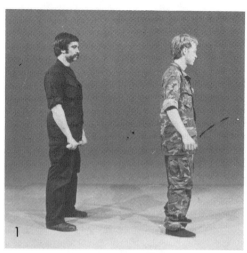

NECK STRIKE WITH A STRAIGHT CHOKE APPLIED WITH THE BATON IN CONJUNCTION WITH A DROPPING BACK BREAKER TO THE KNEE

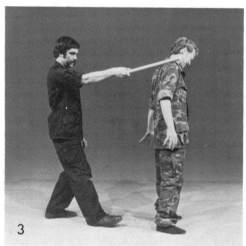

OUTSIDE LOWER LEG STRIKE, ANKLE SWEEP WITH THE BATON AND DOUBLE LEG CONTROL

2

4

5

7

CHAPTER TWO

THE SHORT STICK

The *SHORT STICK* or double short stick, can be measured between 12 inches and 30 inches in length. Due to its short length, the short stick provides a rapid method of striking, and creates an added extension to the stick fighter's arm and hand during close-combat encounters. Fast and hard, the short stick is directed against nerve centers and bony portions of the enemy's anatomy. Usually executed with *short striking-hard shocking technique*, the *double short stick* can strike multiple targets in a minimum of reaction time, at a much closer interval than the baton. This is not to say that the short stick outweighs the baton in combat situations, it just implies that it is used at a different interval with a different rhythm of attack.

In the following chapter, I will focus upon the use of the Short-Stick, and Double Short-Stick in the following categories:

1. Basic methods of striking, chokings, takedowns and controls

2. Armbars, joint-locks and defense against armed attacks

3. Methods of disarming the stick once it has been grasped by the assailant.

Remember, all the basic blocks, strikes and techniques of the baton can be used with small variations with the short stick, double short stick, or any other length of stick available to the combat soldier. All weapons are essentially the same to the weapons expert, once he has attained that *body/mind* extension of *feel* and *energy transference* into the hand-held weapon. Refer to page 25, and the basic method of self-hypnosis, for mind/body/weapon familiarization and awareness.

**DOUBLE SHORT STICKS/
WRIST STRIKE AND BLOCK
AGAINST A KNIFE THRUST
WITH THE STICK FIGHTER'S
LEFT HAND, RIGHT HAND
TO THE TEMPLE, LEFT-
HAND STRIKE TO THE
BRIDGE OF THE NOSE
WITH A RIGHT-HAND STRIKE
TO THE RIGHT LOWER
KNEECAP OF THE ATTACKER**

2

3

5

6

9

10

DIRECT SIDE STEP WITH A
RIGHT-HAND STRIKE TO THE
ATTACKER'S KNIFEHAND,
LEFT-HAND STRIKE TO THE
LOWER LEG AND KNEECAP,
A TURNING RIGHT-HAND
STRIKE TO THE TEMPLE
WITH A SLIDING
TWO-HANDED STRAIGHT
CHOKE WITH THE BATON

99

TWO-HANDED ELBOW BLOCK
WITH THE BATON TO THE
ENEMY'S ATTACKING
KNIFEHAND, RIGHT-HAND
STRAIGHT THRUST TO
THE EDGE, LEFT-HANDED
ELBOW STRIKE TO THE TEMPLE,
A NECK TRAP WITH A LOW
LEG SWEEP FOLLOWED BY AN
OVERHAND DOWNSTRIKE TO
THE TOP OF THE HEAD

2

4

5

7

CONTINUED

8

11

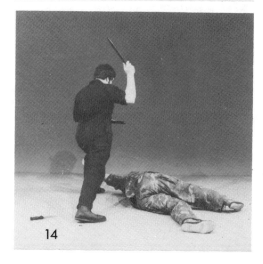

14

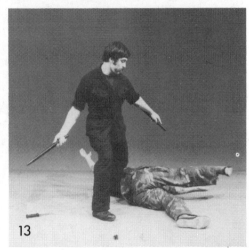

SINGLE SHORT STICK
LEFT-HANDED BLOCK, TRAP
AND CONTROL, A RIGHT-
HANDED STRIKE TO THE
BRIDGE OF THE NOSE,
SHOOT-BEHIND
SLEEPER CHOKE WITH
A DROPPING
BACK BREAKER

1

4

5

8

9

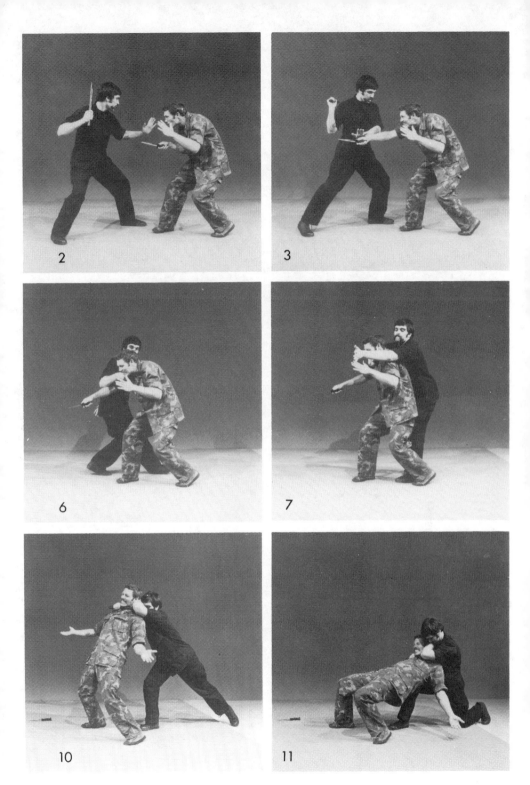

LEFT-HANDED ELBOW STRIKE,
RIGHT-HANDED KNEE STRIKE,
LEFT-HANDED THROAT STRIKE,
A DROPPING 360-DEGREE LOW
LEG SWEEP WITH AN OUTSIDE
CIRCULAR STRIKE TO THE
CLAVICLE

2

4

5

7

CONTINUED

8

11

14

9

10

12

13

15

SINGLE SHORT STICK/ TWO-HANDED OUTSIDE CIRCULAR ARM BAR, TAKEDOWN AND CONTROL

2

3

6

7

10

11

111

HIGH-RISING HAND BLOCK AND ARM BAR, CROSS-LEG REAPING THROW TAKEDOWN AND CONTROL WITH AN ELBOW LOCK

1

4

7

8

2

3

5

6

9

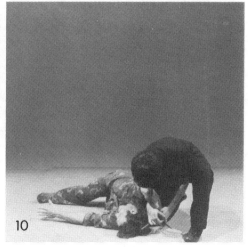

10

113

**LEFT-HANDED BLOCK
AND TRAP AGAINST
A KNIFE ATTACK,
RIGHT-HANDED ELBOW STRIKE,
TAKEDOWN AND CONTROL
WITH AN ARM BAR APPLIED
AGAINST THE ELBOW**

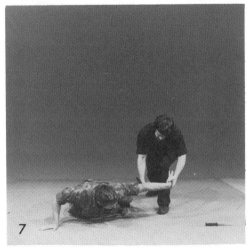

LEFT-HANDED STRIKE
TO THE ATTACKER'S
KNIFEHAND, RIGHT-HANDED
LOW STRIKE TO THE KNEE,
360-DEGREE OUTSIDE
CIRCULAR WHIPPING BLOW
TO THE BACK OF THE NECK,
180-DEGREE TURNING
DOWNSTRIKE TO THE HEAD

CONTINUED

10

12

15

11

13

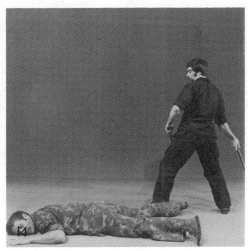

14

119

DEFENSE AGAINST
A ONE-HANDED GRASP
ON A SINGLE SHORT STICK,
OUTSIDE CIRCULAR WRIST LOCK
WITH THE BATON, TAKEDOWN
AND KNEE THRUST
TO THE FACE

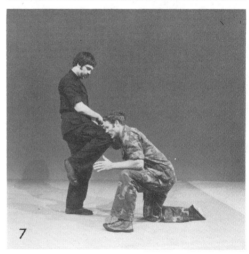

120

DEFENSE AGAINST
A TWO-HANDED
GRASP OF THE SHORT STICK,
360-DEGREE OUTSIDE SPIN WITH
A DROPPING LEG SWEEP,
BREAKAWAY NECK STRIKE
AND CONTROL

CHAPTER THREE

THE SNAPPING SHORT STICK "BONE BREAKER"

This amazing little weapon of self-defense, must be considered one of the most economical—totally effective methods of protection available.

Considered the *OLD MAN'S* tool of self-defense, the Snapping Short Stick is a totally deceptive weapon. Approximately 11 inches in length, and one inch in diameter, and made of oak, the bone breaker is used in short, shocking strikes against bony portions of the anatomy and for paralyzing nerve centers. Once contact is made on a bony protrusion of the enemy's anatomy, the bone breaker shatters the bone, much as a rock hitting a windshield of a car at high speed. The length and width of the weapon form a tool similar to a *tuning fork*, creating vibrations as the oak stick makes contact with another object. These vibrations enter the bone and create a shattering effect upon contact, totally disabling the attacker's portion of his anatomy as it enters your sphere of defense.

The hand cord attached to the butt of the weapon creates a release-retraction method, not available in other methods of self-defense, such as the *fan* or *yawari stick*. The bone breaker can be snapped out and retracted quickly by use of the cord attached to the weapon. And wrapped over the thumb and outside of the weapon-hand, it creates an added snap and shock to the initial strikes.

The following chapter will be demonstrated by Charles Sanders and Randy Warner, a close friend of ours, and a hwa rang do instructor for Joo Bang Lee. The following techniques will be done in these categories:

1. Grasping the stick   4. Combinations and takedowns
2. Blocking   5. Choking and control.
3. Striking

This fascinating weapon is extremely deceptive, and great caution should be taken during its training and use.

At close quarters in crowded or tight areas where the baton becomes restricted because of interval, the bone breaker exceeds all forms of defensive close-quarter combatives aimed at controlling the assailant.

All fighting techniques of the stick are combined with striking, kicking, joint locking and throwing or choking as they are with all 108 weapons of hwa rang do and its unarmed systems of close combat.

BONE BREAKER/ THE STRAP OF
THE BONE BREAKER IS PLACED
OVER THE THUMB,
SWUNG OUTSIDE
AND UP INTO THE HAND,
RETRACTED BACK
AND SNAPPED FORWARD IN
A SHOCKING SNAPPING
STRIKING MOTION

127

**HIGH-RISING
HIGH BLOCK**

**RIGHT-HANDED
OUTSIDE BLOCK**

**RIGHT-HANDED
INSIDE BLOCK**

3

4

5

**RIGHT-HANDED
OUTSIDE LOW
BLOCK**

DOWNSTRIKE
TO THE TOP
OF THE HEAD,
COMBINED WITH
A SHORT STRIKE
TO THE TEMPLE

**OUTSIDE
SHORT STRIKE
TO THE TEMPLE
WITH A STRAIGHT
THRUST TO THE
BRIDGE OF
THE NOSE**

STRAIGHT THRUST TO THE THROAT AND BUTT STRIKE TO THE TEMPLE

138

**STRAIGHT THRUST TO THE
EYES, BUTT STRIKE TO
THE COLLARBONE
WITH A CIRCULAR STRIKE
TO THE BRIDGE OF THE NOSE**

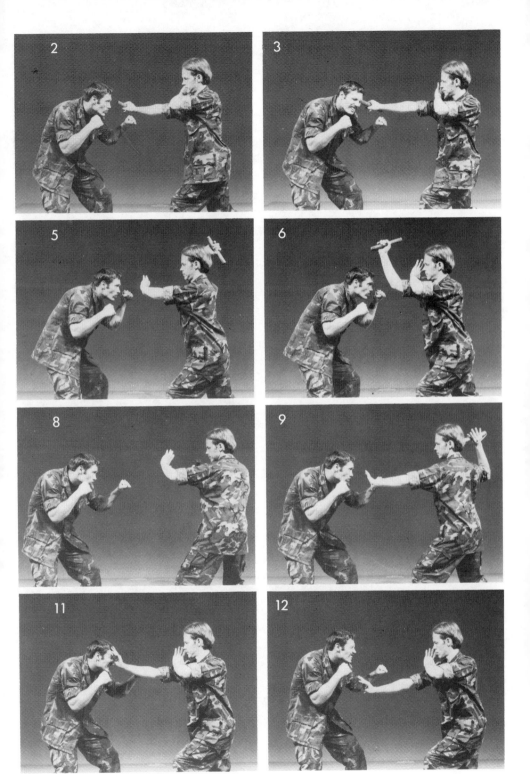

141

**WRIST STRIKE AND BLOCK
AGAINST A KNIFE ATTACK,
A SPINNING LEG STRIKE,
KIDNEY STRIKE, SPINNING
HAIR GRASP AND HEAD STRIKE**

1

4

7

8

2 3

5 6

9 10

CONTINUED

11

14

17

WRIST STRIKE AND BLOCK,
HEAD STRIKE, TEMPLE STRIKE,
COLLARBONE STRIKE, LOW
LEG STRIKE AND SWEEP WITH
A GARMENT GRASP,
SPINNING SPINE STRIKE

2

4

5

7

CONTINUED

8

11

14

9

10

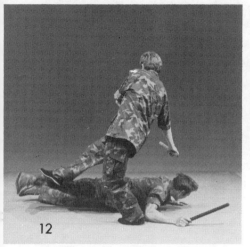

12

13

WRIST STRIKE AND BLOCK, HEAD STRIKE, SPINNING LEG STRIKE, GARMENT GRASP AND REAR LEG SWEEP, DOUBLE DOWN STRIKE

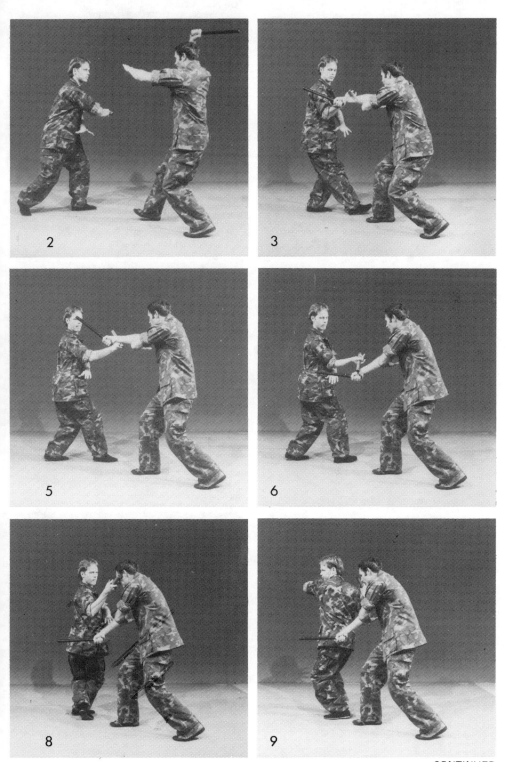

CONTINUED

10

13

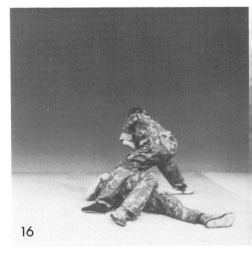

16

11

12

14

15

17

153

WRIST STRIKE AND BLOCK,
HEAD STRIKE, SPINNING GROIN
STRIKE WITH A FOOT SWEEP
AND THRUST TO EYES

4

5

8

9

WRIST STRIKE AND BLOCK,
SPINNING COLLARBONE
STRIKE, THROAT STRIKE,
GARMENT GRASP,
CROSS-LEG REAPING THROW,
STRIKE TO THE JAWBONE

**WRIST STRIKE
AND BLOCK, SPINNING
HEAD STRIKE, BUTT
STRIKE, SINGLE LEG
TAKEDOWN FROM
THE REAR, FOLLOW-UP
STRIKE TO THE SPINE**

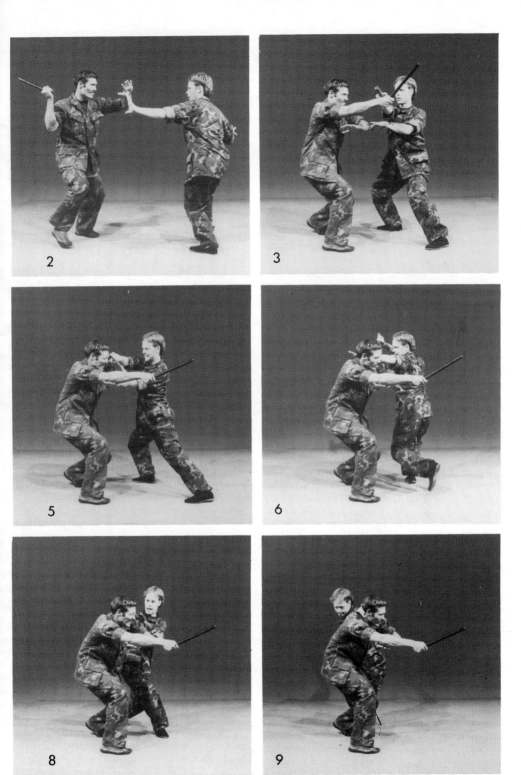

CONTINUED

10

13

16

ELBOW STRIKE AND BLOCK, EYE THRUST, STEP-BEHIND STRAIGHT CHOKE WITH THE SHORT STICK

2

3

6

7

10

11

CHAPTER FOUR

THE CANE

The cane has long been considered the "gentleman's" weapon for self-defense. Often carried by the old and disabled, the cane has been a sign of weakness, and in this deception alone lies a great advantage.

Years ago, in the ancient times of Korea and Asia, the noble class was aware of this advantage for self-defense, so they developed a series of techniques for defense, physical training and exercise. Thus a sign of weakness and deception became a weapon and vehicle of strength for the old and noble.

In actuality the cane is an extremely dangerous weapon, and the curvature of the handle is an excellent tool for blocking, trapping and controlling attacks to the limbs. The hook of the cane provides an excellent point to apply pressure against nerve centers and for choking, tearing or gouging.

Direct thrusts with the tip of the cane are made to vital nerve centers. Primary targets are the eyes, throat, solar plexus and groin. The blocks are utilized as strikes against bony protrusions of the anatomy, followed by a trap and throw, thus the cane becomes an excellent weapon of control and self-defense in critical situations.

These basic cane techniques are demonstrated by my master instructor, the supreme grandmaster of hwa rang do, Joo Bang Lee, to whom this book is dedicated.

1

2

**HIGH BLOCK,
ARM BAR,
TAKEDOWN
AND CONTROL**

3

4

·5

6

**HIGH BLOCK
AND TWISTING
ARM LOCK**

168

3

4

LOW BLOCK, HIGH BLOCK, SHOOT-BEHIND AND GROIN RIP

SIDE STEPPING
HAND TRAP
WITH A
REDIRECTION
INTO THE GROIN
AGAINST A
KNIFE ATTACK
AND DOWNWARD
THRUST

1

2

5

6

1

4

5

**LOW BLOCK, HIGH BLOCK,
WRIST CATCH AND ARM LOCK,
TAKEDOWN AND CONTROL**

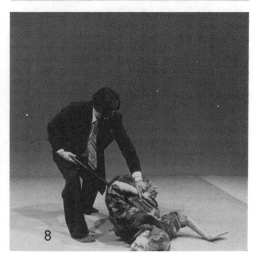

LOW BLOCK, HIGH BLOCK, OUTSIDE CIRCULAR CLAVICLE CATCH, TAKEDOWN AND CONTROL

4

7

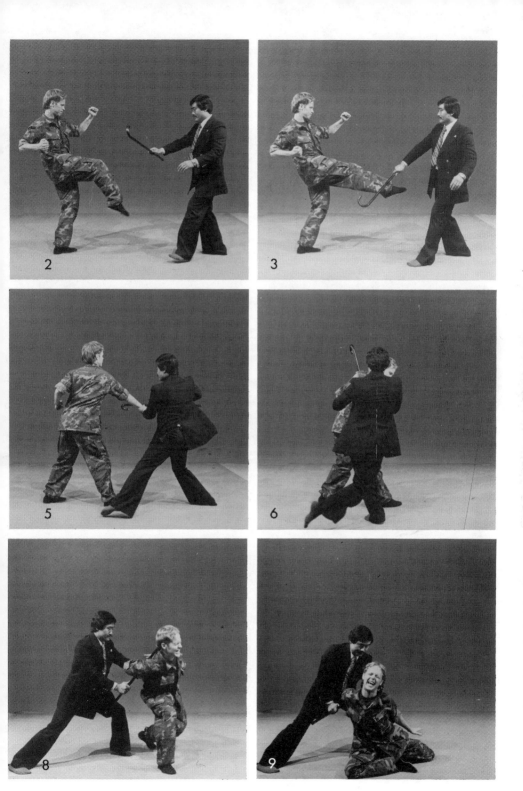

HIGH BLOCK, LOW LEG SWEEP,
SLIDING NECK STRIKE
AND CONTROL

LEFT-HANDED HIGH BLOCK,
NECK CATCH WITH THE CANE,
FORWARD THRUST TO THE
COLLARBONE, TAKEDOWN
AND CONTROL

LEFT-HANDED HIGH BLOCK,
GROIN CATCH WITH A
BACK-DROPPING SWING
THROW AND CONTROL

2

4

5

7

185

**LOW BLOCK, HIGH BLOCK
WRIST LOCK WITH AN
OUTSIDE CIRCULAR WRIST-
BREAKING THROW
AND CONTROL**

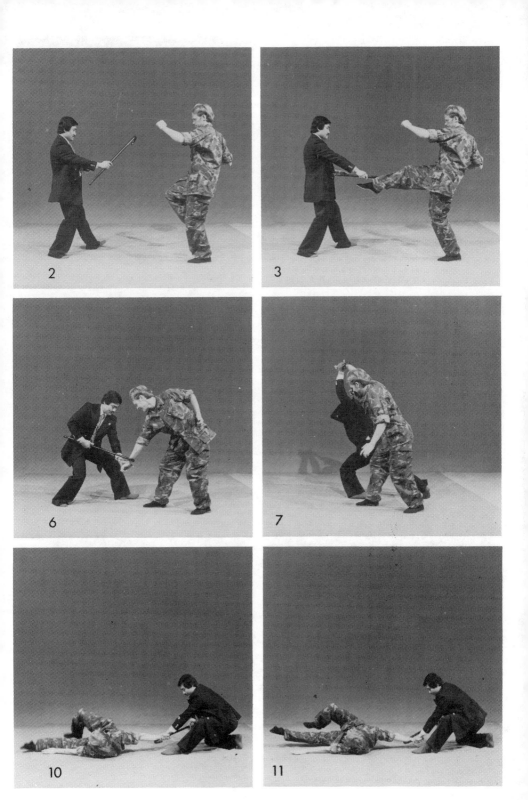

**LOW BLOCK, HIGH BLOCK
WITH A WRIST LOCK AND
INSIDE CIRCULAR WRIST-
BREAKING THROW
AND CONTROL**

1

4

7

8

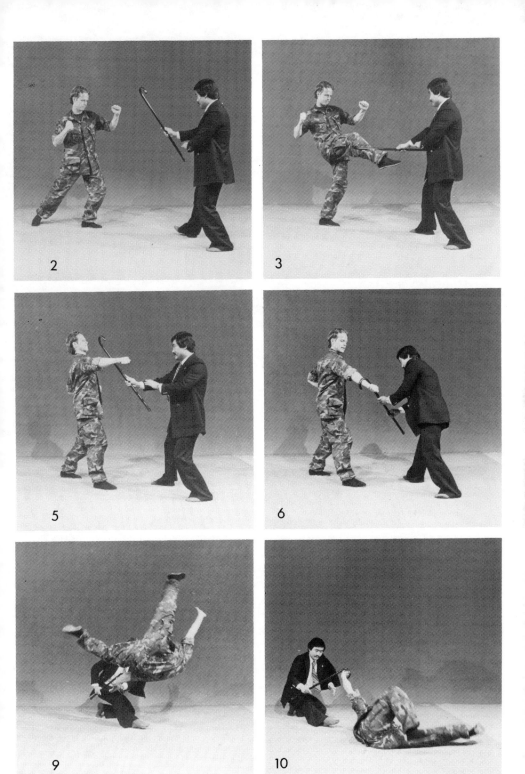

**LOW BLOCK, HIGH BLOCK,
NECK CATCH WITH THE CANE,
INSIDE CIRCULAR NECK-
BREAKING THROW
AND CONTROL**

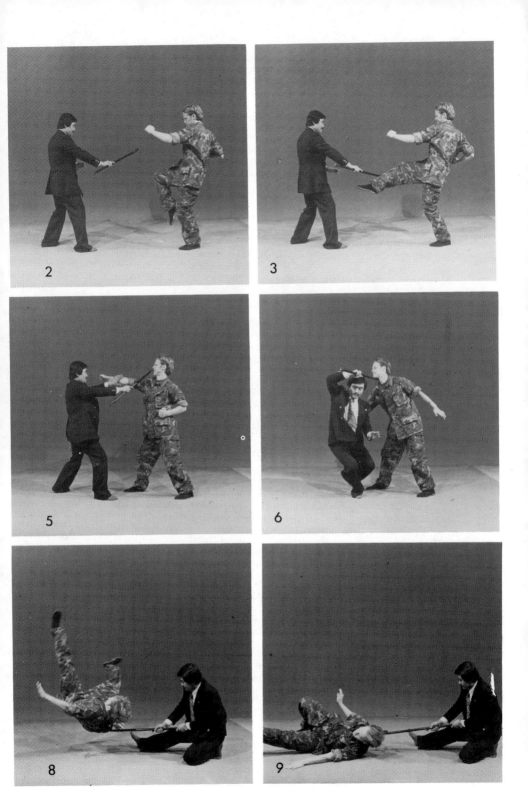

CONCLUSION

Stick Fighting for Combat is essentially the same as any other aspect of hand-to-hand combat. Perfect the basics of attack and counterattack, while focusing the mind upon strategy and reaction. Once thought no longer becomes necessary, then unified reaction will be attained, a conditioned reflex. And with this being your final goal, constant perfection of reaction, you will develop the ability to defend yourself in critical situations.

This book was not written in the context of being the answer to self-defense or stick fighting, but as a basis for your awareness and knowledge, and so that with these basics you may search deep within, discover new variations which conform to your psychological/physical abilities and limitations, and strive to perfect these techniques which are special to you, and with which you feel comfortable. Remember, this book is merely the basics of stick fighting, and by no means is it the answer or the final word. Develop your techniques and train relentlessly.

I have chosen to dwell upon other forms of stick fighting and *not* upon the long staff or Bo staff.

This book is intended for use of all unconventional weapons personnel, police officers and people concerned with common-sense self-defense.

Michael D. Echanis